IT'S ALL ABOUT ME!

HOW TO SURVIVE LIFE WITH A NARCISSIST

BY
MARJORIE SHEPPARD-KNIELE, M.ED

ISBN-10: 1482328291
EAN-13: 9781482328295
Library of Congress Control Number: 2013902032

CreateSpace Independent Publishing Platform
North Charleston, South Carolina

Dedicated to my original editor,
Rebecca O'Boyle, for her insight, support,
intelligence, and love.

CONTENTS

INTRODUCTION

Do You Know Anyone Like This?

✓ Someone who is animated and even charming when the attention is on him, but who is totally bored and uninterested when the light shines on someone else in the room?

✓ Someone who will wrestle every conversation back to focusing on her; *her* life, *her* stories, *her* accomplishments, *her* problems?

✓ Someone who leaves you feeling drained after almost every encounter?

✓ Someone who makes you feel crazy, selfish, frustrated, and confused?

✓ Someone who seems to live by the motto "What's in it for me?"

✓ Someone who is so high-maintenance that he seems to suck the energy from your body?

✓ Someone who sees your good fortune, exciting prospects, and achievements as nothing more than competition?

If you answered yes to more than one of these questions, chances are you have a narcissist in your life. Narcissists have an excessive need for admiration or adulation. They truly believe that in every social situation, it's all about them. At their core, narcissists are takers. They are disconnected from their own feelings and, frankly, have no interest in yours. Narcissists want to know what other people can do for them, and they will deploy any means necessary to get what they want. Developing and nurturing close emotional relationships is not a priority for the narcissist. Getting what they want is the priority, and narcissists can be cunning manipulators and intimidating bullies. They can also be extremely charming, self-effacing, funny, and alluring. Beneath the surface, however, is a person with a hole in his soul. Once you buy into the belief that only *you* can fill the void inside the narcissist, you are snagged. And once snagged, your suffering begins.

I have been where you are, and I now realize that much of my misery, confusion, frustration, and suffering emanated from lack of knowledge about narcissism, as well as from my own belief that I had the power to fix another person. This belief was at the center of my pain and was directly responsible for my choosing and staying in relationships that were clearly not good for me.

In writing this book, my intention was to simply share some of what I have learned with a modicum of hope that if even one person can benefit from my experiences, I have accomplished my goal. I have come to know that the world can be a beautiful, loving, soft place. But it was up to me to create this new reality. The narcissists in my life are still narcissistic. I pray for them, but I strongly suspect that they will never change. Eleanor Roosevelt once said, "No one can make you feel inferior without your consent." I have learned to stop giving my consent—will you?

CHAPTER 1

Mary's Story

**The hole loomed large before her,
but she just didn't see it!**

I remember the first moment I met Will. To this day, it brings a smile to my face. The way he looked at me! It was as if I had been hypnotized! During our first weeks together, I was astounded that Will seemed to know my very soul and wanted nothing more than to make every dream of mine come true. He would tell me that I was the most loving person he had ever met. He seemed to want what I wanted. I would often think "this is what is meant by a soul-mate." Over candlelit, romantic dinners and walks in the moonlight, he would talk about how he would one day make lots of money and build our dream home. He said our future would be filled with exotic trips and a big family. I was drawn completely to this "home-loving" provider. He asked me to help him learn to love fully so he could become a better person. He called me his "love teacher." If I am honest, I remember feeling very powerful and desired. It was like a drug! I knew I could teach him to love. He had had a troubled childhood, but it would be OK because I was here now and I would teach him to trust and to open up. I would fill that empty hole inside of him.

Will was recently divorced and had two little boys. He told me that he was seldom able to see his sons because his ex-wife started fights and it upset the children. He never missed an opportunity to compare me to his ex and tell me how different I was from her. He often said that he wished he was more aware when he married her, but alas, they were young and she was pregnant, so they had to get married. He loved his sons desperately, but it was easier on them if they didn't see their parents fighting all the time, so he didn't push to see them. His ex-wife was also money-hungry and demanded exorbitant child-support payments. Will said that he knew she had just bought a new car, got to keep the beautiful house, and had a boyfriend who had lots of money. I was amazed that although he had been treated so badly, he always smiled and had such faith in me as a person and us as a couple.

I knew he had gotten a raw deal in the past, but with us, everything would be different. He asked me to marry him only three months after we met. I told everyone I was swept off my feet, that I had met "Mr. Right," so why should we wait?

Examining Mary's Thought Patterns

Let's make believe that Mary is willing to critically evaluate her romance with Will. She asks you to give her some feedback about the potential problems she may be overlooking in her new and exciting romance. (*Note:* There is virtually *no* chance that Mary would actually ask for this feedback. The *high* she is experiencing feels too good at the moment. Nonetheless, let's pretend.) See if you can spot some of the red flags:

> *[Will] would tell me that he needed to learn how to love and that I was the most loving person he had ever met.*

1. Will tells Mary that he needs to learn to love. What concerns you about this statement?

2. Will tells Mary that she is the most loving person he has ever met. List the ways in which this is disturbing to you. (Hint: they have just met.)

> *He asked me to help him learn to love fully*
> *so he could become a better person.*

1. Will asks Mary to help him become a better person. Is this Mary's responsibility or Will's?
2. Are you sensing any "danger" signals for Mary here?

> *He called me his "love teacher." If I'm honest, I remember feeling*
> *very powerful and desired. It was like a drug! I knew I could*
> *teach him to love. He had had a troubled childhood, but it*
> *would be OK because I was here now and I would teach him to*
> *trust and to open up. I would fill that empty hole inside of him.*

1. What do you think Mary's needs are, based on what you know so far?
2. Why do you think Will's requests are like a "drug" to her?
3. Pay attention to Mary's choice of words when she describes herself in relation to her early relationship with Will (e.g., powerful, desired).

> *He told me that he was seldom able to see his sons because his*
> *ex-wife started fights and it upset the children.*

1. Will is not seeing much of his children. How much responsibility is Will taking for this?
2. Could there be any other explanations for Will's distancing from his children?

> *He never missed an opportunity to compare me to his ex and tell me how different I was from her.*

1. Think about Mary's needs and her susceptibility when Will compares her to his first wife. Do you get the sense that Mary likes this comparison?
2. With the dynamic of "con artist" and "mark" in mind, describe Will and Mary.
3. Assuming Mary would listen, what feedback might have helped Mary here?

> *He loved his sons desperately, but it was easier on them if they didn't see their parents fighting all the time, so he didn't push to see them.*

1. What is your gut reaction to this statement by Will?
2. How do you think his sons are interpreting his absence?

His ex-wife was also money-hungry and demanded exorbitant child-support payments. Will said that he knew she had just bought a new car, got to keep the beautiful house, and had a boyfriend who had lots of money. I was amazed that although he had been treated so badly, he always smiled and had such faith in me as a person and us as a couple.

1. How do Will's complaints register with you?
2. What does this tell you about Will's willingness to take responsibility for his part in the failure of his marriage?
3. What is Will's past behavior telling you about what kind of father he might make if he and Mary have a family of their own?

During our first weeks together, I was astounded that Will seemed to know my very soul and wanted nothing more than to make every dream of mine come true. He seemed to want what I wanted.

1. Does this all seem a little too good to be true?
2. How does Mary's assessment that "he seemed to want what I wanted" strike you?

He said our future would be filled with exotic trips and a big family. I was drawn completely to this "home-loving" provider.

1. How does Will's desire for a big family mesh with the fact that he already *has* a family?
2. How do you think Will plans to take care of his two sons once he has more children with Mary?
3. If Mary was listening to her *inner-knower*, what would the warnings be about this choice of a father for her children?

> *I knew he had gotten a raw deal, but I thought that everything would be different with us. He asked me to marry him only three months after we met. I told everyone I was swept off my feet; that I had met "Mr. Right," so why should we wait?*

1. What do you think about Mary's determination to make everything better for Will?
2. What patterns are beginning to emerge here?
3. What are your thoughts regarding Will and Mary getting married after knowing each other for only three months?

If Mary's story sounds familiar, perhaps you are beginning to consider the possibility that you and Mary have something in common. You seem to choose love relationships where you are excited by the opportunity to *give* to someone in need.

We'll follow Mary's relationship with Will throughout this book. We'll talk about stages in the context of healthy emotional development. And we'll talk about patterns. The more skilled you become at recognizing these patterns, the more likely you'll be able to spot danger and eventually take responsibility for your part in creating and sustaining destructive patterns. As you read through this book and follow Mary and Will's relationship, try to connect with Mary's needs, behaviors, and thinking patterns. With the advantage of objectivity and distance, you may be in a better position to see the comparison between you and Mary, and to gain some clarity regarding your own story and possible flaws in your own *choosing mechanism*.

Mary and Will: Five Years Later

Well, Mary did marry Will, after a whirlwind courtship, flowers, long walks in the park, and romantic dinners. Let's take a look at their marriage now, five years later:

The day I married Will was perhaps the happiest day of my life. We bought a lovely little home that actually had a white picket fence. I decorated a beautiful room for Will's sons and couldn't wait to meet them and begin our new family. In many ways, it was like coming home for me. I had seen pictures of Will's sons, and they reminded me of my twin brothers when they were that age. They were adorable. Unfortunately, Will's little boys were not so excited to meet me. They clung to Will and refused to move from one spot in the living room. I knew I had to give them time to get to know me, but their visits were so sporadic and short-lived that we were never really able to develop any kind of relationship.

Will also seemed to be having trouble adjusting to our new relationship. After the honeymoon, he seemed to change. He became withdrawn and moody. When I tried to get close, he would stiffen and tell me he had a lot on his mind. He also started picking on little things I did. As I look back, his comments were characterized by how disappointed he was in me and how I wasn't living up to his expectations. When I tried to talk to him about anything, he would tell me I was too "clingy and insecure" and he "needed space"; once he said I was acting like his first wife! "I didn't think you were like this," he'd say. "While we were dating you were so much easier to be with, more independent and carefree." I was shocked. I didn't know what had changed, but I knew it had to be something I was doing. Maybe I had spent too much time decorating our new home instead of giving Will special attention. Maybe I wasn't doting on him the way I did when we were dating. Maybe he was sad about not being able to see his boys. When I tried to talk to him about it, he would roll his eyes and say, "God, here we go again. You are so high maintenance! I just didn't see this before we got married." I learned to stay quiet. I didn't want him to think I was dependent, but I was feeling insecure and afraid and, ironically, more dependent than I had ever felt in my life! I tried and tried to change in ways that would please him, but he seemed so unhappy with me: cold and distant.

The only time Will wanted to be near me was during sex. He was his old self again when he got in the mood. He would tease me and tickle me and whisper how much he loved me. I lived for these times. Even when I wasn't in the mood, I would never say no because this was the only time I got to hold Will and he would hold me. For a while, he would be happy and loving, but soon the world would impose on him, and I would feel the distance again. I wished there was something I could do to make his life happy all the time.

Now it's been almost five years since we've been married, and I have never felt worse about myself. I look around at other happy couples and feel like a total loser. For the most part, I keep out of Will's way and try to help him as much as I can with his sons and his anger toward his first wife. When the boys do come over, Will lies on the couch and the boys play on the computer or text their friends. The boys are teenagers now and, like most teenagers, they are sullen and withdrawn. When all three of them are in the house, it is a lonely and frustrating place for me to be. No one talks. The boys can't wait till it is time to go home, and when Will comes back after dropping them off he is more miserable and hostile than ever. He says he hates his ex-wife for having turned his sons against him. He often comments about his disappointment in them too, saying they're turning out just like her. I know to keep my mouth shut, especially during these times. If I am totally honest, I am very lonely and don't know how to improve my marriage. There must be some way to break through to Will. But as the years pass, I have less and less confidence about being successful at this.

Exploring Mary's Beliefs After Five Years of Marriage to Will

> *As I look back, his comments were characterized by how disappointed he was in me and how I wasn't living up to his expectations. I didn't know what had changed, but I knew it had to be something I was doing.*

1. What are Mary's conclusions about Will's unhappiness?
2. What conclusions does Mary draw from Will's verbal attacks?

> *Maybe I had spent too much time decorating our new home instead of giving Will special attention. Maybe I wasn't doting on him the way I did when we were dating. Maybe he was sad about not being able to see his boys.*

1. Who is responsible (in Mary's mind) for the problems in her marriage?
2. Who is responsible (in Mary's mind) to fix the problems?
3. What is Mary's assessment of the drastic changes in Will after they were married?
4. Notice how Mary's sense of self (and her happiness) is determined by how Will treats her on a given day.

> *I wished there was something I could do to make his life happy all the time....I look around at other happy couples and feel like a total loser.*

1. How would you describe Mary at this point in her marriage?
2. Elaborate on Mary's beliefs about responsibility.
3. When Mary observes other happy couples, who does she hold accountable for her unhappiness? What does this tell you about her beliefs?

> *The boys can't wait till it is time to go home, and when Will comes back after dropping them off he is more miserable and hostile than ever. He says he hates his ex-wife for having turned his sons against him. He often comments about his disappointment in them too, saying they're turning out just like her.*

1. Describe some of Will's beliefs about his life and the way things have turned out for him.
2. In Will's mind, who is responsible for the distance he feels in his relationship with his sons?
3. What is Will doing about his relationship with his sons?

> *If I am totally honest, I am very lonely and don't know how to improve my marriage. There must be some way to break through to Will. But as the years pass, I have less and less confidence about being successful at this.*

1. Describe how Mary is feeling at this time in her life.
2. What do you think will become of Mary if she continues on this path?

The Formation of Mary's Beliefs: Mary's Family of Origin

Mary's mother, Lynette, was only eighteen (and pregnant) when she married Mary's father, Jim. Lynette and Jim had six children by the time they were thirty. Mary was the couple's fourth child, and she was five when her younger brothers (twins) were born.

Mary's older brothers were the biggest, toughest kids in the neighborhood. They were often in trouble, getting into fights, getting suspended from school, or being punished for their grades. Mary's older sister was distant and cool toward her. If she spoke to Mary at all, it was to tell her to get lost or stop touching her things.

When the twins were born, Mary felt that she had finally found her place in the family. She loved the babies instantly and felt that they were hers to care for, and her mother actually seemed grateful for Mary's help. "Mary, go get a diaper for me; Mary give this bottle to your brother. You're a good sister," her mother would say, "Mama's little helper." Lynette was often in bed or lying on the couch. Mary knew her mother was sad most of the time, and being able to help meant everything and made Mary feel special. Now instead of being the lost child with nothing to offer, she was suddenly a capable, helpful, and loving daughter.

As she grew, Mary became remarkably competent at housekeeping and child care. By the time she was nine, she was the primary caretaker for her little brothers. She would rush home from school to take the twins off her mother's hands. Sometimes her mother even allowed her to miss school because she was tired and needed Mary's help. Mary's father would often comment that Mary would make some lucky man a good wife one day. She would live for these compliments and make sure that the house was clean, the table set, and dinner on the stove when her father came home from work. Lynette had never been a good housekeeper, which was a constant source of friction between her and Jim. But Mary was good at these things, good at cleaning and caring for her dad folding his socks and lining them up in the drawers just the way he liked. She began to take on more and more responsibility around the house while her father worked and her mother stayed in bed or lay on the couch. The three older children were seldom home, and Mary loved it when she had the house to herself—her little brothers clean and cared for, the house in order, and her father on his way home.

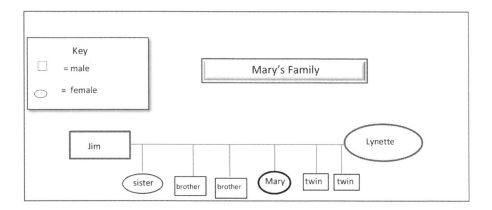

Exploring Mary's Early Childhood

Beliefs form early in life. Let's inspect some of the relationships within Mary's family and the expectations Mary's parents had for her. You will start to see beliefs being formed in young Mary's life that proved to be dangerous to her later in life, when she met Will and others like him.

> *When the twins were born, Mary felt that she had finally found her place in the family. She loved them instantly and felt that they were hers to care for, and her mother actually seemed grateful for Mary's help. Now, instead of being the lost child with nothing to offer, she was suddenly a capable, helpful, and loving daughter.*

1. What would you guess Mary's beliefs were about her status in the family before the twins were born?
2. What needs did the twin infants fill in Mary?

> *"Mary, go get a diaper for me; Mary, give this bottle to your brother. You're such a good sister,"* her mother would say, *"Mama's little helper."* Lynette was often in bed or lying on the couch. Mary knew her mother was sad most of the time, and being able to help meant everything to her and made her feel special.*

1. How did Lynette contribute to a pattern of caretaking in her daughter?
2. What do you think was happening to Lynette emotionally?
3. Was Lynette's sadness and depression Mary's responsibility?
4. Do you think Mary felt that it was her responsibility?

> *As she grew, Mary became remarkably competent at housekeeping and child care. By the time she was nine, she was the primary caretaker for her little brothers. She would rush home from school, and sometimes her mother even allowed her to miss school because she was tired and needed Mary's help. Mary's father would often comment that Mary would make some lucky man a good wife one day.*

1. How did Jim contribute to this pattern of caretaking in his daughter?

2. What messages was Mary receiving from her parents?
3. What about school or Mary's social life? Whose needs were emerging as foremost here?

Lynette had never been a good housekeeper, which was a constant source of friction between her and Jim. But Mary was good at these things, good at cleaning and caring for her dad folding his socks and lining them up in the drawers, just the way he liked.

---

1. Can you see a triangle emerging with Mary, Jim, and Lynette?
2. What beliefs might Mary have been forming about approval from men and from women?
3. What beliefs might Mary have been forming about competition with women for a man's approval?
4. Finally, fast forward again to Mary's marriage to Will. Can you see how the beliefs she formed as a child were similar to those she had as a married woman?

CHAPTER 2:

Will's Story: A Look at How Narcissists See the World

While reading about Mary, did you wonder what was going on inside Will's head? Did you wonder about *his* beliefs, *his* childhood? Because Will is a good example of a narcissist, telling his story is important only in as much as it shines a light on how he thinks and how his beliefs may have been formed. Most importantly, Will's story highlights how difficult it can be to have an honest, intimate relationship with a person like him. Will is charming, articulate, cunning, and intelligent. At the beginning of a relationship, he presents himself as the most insightful, kind, and loving person. He doesn't outright lie, but he "spins" the truth in order to win you over. He is masterful. Underlying this performance, however, is a person who really trusts no one. He is a wounded soul who will never allow himself to feel true vulnerability. Will believes that to be vulnerable is to be weak, and ultimately weak people are annihilated. So as you become open and vulnerable, he becomes increasingly judgmental of your "weaknesses."

The Formation of Will's Beliefs

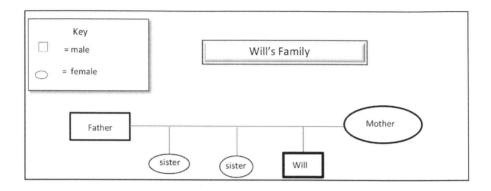

My father lived in the house with me, my mother, and my two older sisters, but he might as well have been dead. In fact, I think it would have been easier for me if he were dead. As long as I can remember, my father hated my mother and she him. When she wasn't insulting him, she was ignoring him. I was the youngest and learned from my sisters that it was great sport to make fun of my father behind his back (in collusion with my mother) or to totally ignore him. He had no power. Power was held exclusively by my mother. I didn't care what he thought of my grades or my achievement in sports. He simply didn't matter.

I thought this was normal until I began to spend time with other families. None of my friends' fathers were like mine. Every other boy I knew was afraid of his dad: afraid to disappoint him, afraid of being punished, or afraid of not getting his approval. Every father in the neighborhood loomed large in the eyes of their family. He was the central figure around whom the family orbited. My father was an extra cast member.

When my mother wasn't in earshot, my father would mumble terrible things to me. "Come here, little mama's boy," or "Get your head out of your mother's ass and be a man!" Most of the time, he was drunk and out of work.

To make matters worse, my mother hovered over me. She made no bones about the fact that I was her precious little boy. She had always wanted a son. She told her stories over and over. "I've never had time for other women, and frankly I didn't know what to do with little girls. I find them whiny and self-centered," she would say in front of my sisters. "I've always preferred boys."

So this was the world in which I grew up. My father hated me, my sisters were jealous of me (and tortured me constantly), and my mother put me up on a pedestal (which made my sisters hate me even more.) My life was an obstacle course. I was always on the alert. I learned to bob and weave and figure out ways to survive. Women were all-powerful, and I learned to figure out the needs of each one of them. My oldest sister loved chocolate, so I would always find a way to have a chocolate bar for her in my reserves. My other sister was particularly vicious. I learned that the best way to keep her as an ally was to criticize my mother and gossip about her. I would tell her stories about peeking at my mother when she was getting dressed and seeing her huge, saggy boobs and her big fat stomach. She loved those stories, and for a while she was sort of like my friend. At least she didn't torture me.

To sum up the dynamics during my childhood: my sisters hated my mother, my mother adored me, my sisters resented and tortured me, and we all hated my father.

Exploring Will's Early Childhood

When [my mother] wasn't insulting [my father], she was ignoring him. I was the youngest and learned from my sisters that it was great sport to make fun of my father behind his back (in collusion with my mother) or to totally ignore him.

1. List some of the beliefs Will was forming about women, masculinity, and fatherhood.
2. Will was the only other male in the family besides his father. What do you think of his father's behavior?
3. How do you think it felt to live in the environment that was Will's childhood?

> *Women were all-powerful, and I learned to figure out the needs of each one of them.*

1. Will lived in a house full of hostile women, all of whom had considerable power over him. Does any of his behavior make more sense now?
2. Do you get the sense that little Will believed his very survival was at stake? (Hint: "I don't want to end up being treated like my father is treated.")

Will's Adult Beliefs

Will's beliefs about women played a key role in his behavior toward them when he became a man. He was astounded that girls were so easily manipulated when he started dating. He had an uncanny ability to figure them out immediately. He knew what they wanted, and he gave it to them. He was generous with compliments and gifts. Although he always had a girlfriend, he had a wandering eye and was always on the lookout for something better. He was a heartbreaker. In adulthood, he attracted desirable women like bees to pollen. He had no real male friends, seeing other guys as clumsy, dense, and pathetic. He spent lots of time hanging out with men, playing sports and drinking at bars, but when these guys went home to their wives and girlfriends, Will went home alone or with a woman he picked up, who would surely be escorted out the door at sunrise.

Guys admired Will. He was *the man*! They wondered how this guy, who wasn't particularly attractive or wealthy, attracted the most gorgeous women. They idolized his exploits, and many wished they could be like him. But underneath it all, Will was still the little boy who was hated by his father and tortured by his sisters. "These guys are so stupid, they just don't see the real me. Everyone is so easily fooled," he would think. Looking at Will's early life, imagine what beliefs this little boy was developing about women, about men, about relationships, and about his place in the world. Here's Will's own account of his first marriage:

A Peek into the Thinking of a Narcissist

When I was in the prime of my life, my girlfriend got pregnant. I figured I would do the "right" thing and marry her. Why not? She was beautiful and adored me. I walked on water. She was also carrying my son, and I entertained the idea that maybe I could be a good dad (unlike my asshole father). My kid would look up to me! But it didn't take long before my wife became needy and demanding. I felt trapped and knew early on in the marriage that I had made a terrible mistake. My wife, who was once a knockout, got fat and could barely move. In all honesty, I found her disgusting. And she wouldn't leave me alone! She seemed to think that being pregnant made her some kind of queen and I was her slave. I felt like running away all the time. Finally, I met Jennifer, and that got me through the entire pregnancy. I found that I could be nicer to my wife if somebody was taking care of my needs for once. Just before my son was born, my wife found out about the affair. She went nuts—screaming, crying, threatening to kill herself. I thought I had died and gone to hell! I mean c'mon! OK, I screwed up, but her antics were over the top. I lied to her and told her I would end the affair, and then I told Jennifer we had to cool it for a while, just to get my maniac wife off my back. When my son was born, it was like a miracle. I loved that kid and wanted to be a good dad. For a while, all I wanted was to spend time with this little guy, but my wife would nag constantly, "Don't be so rough with him. Be careful. Give him to me!" Finally, I said screw it and called Jennifer. My wife was so wrapped up in the kid that life was pretty good for a while. In fact, she didn't even seem to notice me, so my little affair with Jennifer was good for both of us. Then boom! She was pregnant again! What a mess! After my second son was born, my wife found out about Jennifer again, and this time I just walked out. I mean, why even bother? She took no responsibility for the break-up; she just kept calling me a lying, cheating, bastard. She got herself a good lawyer and took just about everything I had. What a bitch!

Exploring How Will Thinks

When observing Will's beliefs, notice how often he frames his experiences only in terms of how *he* is affected.

I figured I would do the "right" thing and marry her. Why not? She was beautiful and adored me. I walked on water. She was also carrying my son, and I entertained the idea that maybe I could be a good dad (unlike my asshole father). My kid would look up to me!

1. With as much objectivity as possible, try to look at Will's point of view. What matters to him? What do you think he wants? List some of the reasons he may be happy right now. Can you list one or two of his beliefs about relationships?
2. Now, look a little deeper at his words "I entertained the idea that maybe I could be a good dad (unlike my asshole father). My kid would look up to me!" Comment on this.

It didn't take long before my wife became needy and demanding. I felt trapped and knew early on in the marriage that I had made a terrible mistake. My wife, who was once a knockout, got fat and could barely move. In all honesty, I found her disgusting. And she wouldn't leave me alone!

---

1. Comment on Will's statement, "She wouldn't leave me alone" in relation to his relationship with his mother.
2. Will is a man now. Describe his perceptions and his beliefs about his father. Can you see any connections or fears of Will's that may be connected to his father?
3. Does Will's wife remind him of anyone? (Hint: "…peeking at my mother when she was getting dressed and seeing her huge, saggy boobs and her big fat stomach.")

Finally, I met Jennifer, and that got me through the entire pregnancy. I found that I could be nicer to my wife if somebody was taking care of my needs for once.

---

1. This is a key statement about Will's beliefs and his inability to have any degree of empathy for his wife. List the ways in which you can see how futile it may be for Will and his wife to have an intimate, loving, compassionate, relationship at this point in his life.
2. If you have ever had a relationship with someone like Will, take time to write as much as you can about this statement. It is very important!

> *Just before my son was born, my wife found out about the affair. She went nuts—screaming, crying, threatening to kill herself. I thought I had died and gone to hell! I mean c'mon! OK, I screwed up, but her antics were over the top.*

1. List the ways in which Will takes responsibility for the pain he has caused his wife.
2. In your opinion, will ending the affair with Jennifer solve the problems in Will's marriage? If not, why?
3. How hopeful are you that this relationship can be healed?

> *When my son was born, it was like a miracle. I loved that kid and wanted to be a good dad. For a while, all I wanted was to spend time with this little guy, but my wife would nag constantly.*

1. Do you see a glimmer of possibility for Will here? Describe your feelings and thoughts.
2. Consider Will's sons and what they might learn from their Dad.
3. Can you see how patterns might repeat themselves through the generations?

CHAPTER 3:

Carl's Story:
My Family Is Perfect,
It Must Be Me

At this point, you may be thinking, "Wait a minute! Whatever problems I may have in relationships, could not possibly be connected to my family of origin. In fact, my upbringing was nothing like Mary or Will's. In fact, my family could have invented the word "normal.""

Nonetheless, you are in pain and you are looking for answers. Take some time and read Carl's story. Perhaps his story will resonate with yours on some level.

> *As I look back over my childhood years, I have to say that I was a pretty confident kid. I came from what some might consider "the perfect family." My Dad worked really hard and made a lot of money. As a result, my brothers and I were well cared for and privileged in many ways. We all did well academically and each of us excelled in extra-curricular activities. I was captain of the football team, class president, and always had a part-time job. Although my Dad was seldom home, my mother more than made up for his absence. She helped out at our schools, was president of the PTA, assisted us with our homework, went to my games, and maintained our house, which was by far, the nicest in the neighborhood. When my Dad was around, he was kind and understanding, a great guy.*

I guess you could say I was one of the more popular kids in high school and dated the prettiest girls. So you can imagine how confusing it was when I couldn't adjust to college. For some reason, I became depressed. I began partying, drinking, and smoking a lot of pot.

It was during this hazy, unhappy time, that I met Ashley. Actually, we met at a bar. I liked Ashley, but I can't say there was an instant attraction. Although she was attentive and flirtatious, she wasn't my "type". Then again, what was my type? I was changing. I didn't even recognize myself anymore. Because we hung around with the same crowd, Ashley was always there and soon we became a couple.

It didn't take long before Ashley began making small, critical remarks. She'd say things like "No wonder your previous girlfriend dumped you" and "God, comb your hair once in a while" or "when I first met you, I thought you were adorable, now not so much." Believe it or not, I never defended myself against these hurtful remarks. I guess I believed I deserved to be treated this way. Friends at school would ask, "Why don't you put her in her place? Why do you put up with her abuse?" I knew they were right, but I couldn't seem to snap out of it, or stand up for myself. My life seemed to be spiraling out of control. I was beginning to feel like a loser.

Before long, even I had to admit that I was in an emotionally abusive relationship. But that didn't lead to any change. It was like I was in this hazy funk I couldn't claw my way out of. Most times, I felt I deserved it. At other times, I was furious. But Ashley would say things like "Oh Carl, you are just too sensitive. You have no sense of humor! You used to be fun. I'm outta here. I'm going to the bar where people are fun to be around." I would eventually get dressed and join her. I desperately wanted her approval and often apologized just to get things back on kilter. I hated confrontation, and she was right. I was becoming a drag.

Meanwhile, I was lying to my parents about every-thing. I quit the football team, rarely went to class, and slept well into the afternoon, then partied all night. When my parents did find out that I was failing just about every course, my mother, who was always so calm and reserved screamed and said terrible things to me. She said she knew I was weak like her father; that I was an ungrateful liar. I was stunned. I had never seen that look on her face before. It was scary!

The Formation of Carl's Beliefs

Let's take a look at Carl's "perfect" family from a more objective viewpoint. In this family, it helps to look beyond the parents to intergenerational patterns that may have been forming long before Carl was born.

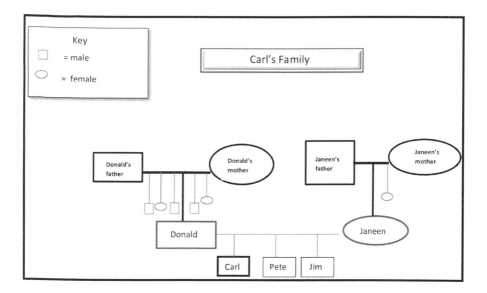

Carl's mother, Janeen, was raised in an alcoholic family. Janeen's father (Carl's grandfather) was a professional who began drinking as soon as he arrived home and all weekend. He often characterized himself as a social drinker, not an alcoholic because he "never missed a day of work." He was a great guy when sober: funny, intelligent, caring, and concerned. But when he was drunk, he was loud, profane, aggressive, and sloppy. As is the case in most alcoholic families, denial was their defense mechanism of choice. Carl's grandmother tried to hide her husband's drinking from the rest of the world. She went to great lengths to paint a picture of the perfect family. While their lives were ridden with confusion, chaos, and turbulence on a daily basis, Janeen's mother didn't seem to notice. One day, Janeen asked about her father's drinking, hoping that her mother could help her in some way with her embarrassment. Her mother snapped and told Janeen that she was ungrateful child who didn't know what it was like to have real problems. She told her that she was lucky to have all the things she had, that many children in the world had much less than her, and to stop complaining. Janeen grew up feeling guilty about her own perceptions, observations, and feelings. Over time, she learned how to cope by adapting a belief that she learned from her mother: Make it look good.

Carl's father, Donald, was raised in a fairly wealthy, upper middle-class family. He had three brothers and two sisters. He often described his home life like army boot camp and his father as a perfectionist who demanded the same from his children. Donald's life was organized and predictable and his mother was the best soldier of all. She kept her children beautifully dressed, maintained her husband's high standards of success, kept a beautiful home, always smiled, and never questioned.

Janeen and Donald met and married in 1985. They were both young and determined to be better parents than they had had. Donald was determined to be the opposite of his "son-of-a-bitch" father. He abhorred anger and avoided it at all costs. His poor mother was a saint, he often said, and he was determined to let his wife run the house and raise the children as she saw fit. As for Janeen, she would make sure that there was no alcohol in her home, for this was the reason her own childhood had been so miserable. This was fine with Donald–whatever made his wife happy. Within a few years they were the proud parents of three beautiful boys, Carl, Pete, and Jim. Because Janeen's upbringing was ridden with secrets and false images, she was determined to be "real". Her home would be transparent. Anyone could walk in at any time and the house was spotless, the boys hair combed and an elaborate dinner simmering on the stove. She helped out at the boys' school, was president of the PTA, assisted them with their homework, and exercised regularly–all the while keeping up a home that could be featured in a magazine. Janeen and Donald were young and energetic. Their sons were remarkably well-behaved and compliant. Their only social life was through their church where they set a great example for everyone.

As the years passed however, life became more difficult, especially when Carl became a teenager. Janeen had no fears about controlling her children as they entered adolescence. All it took was attention, structure, and high expectations. She was a stay-at-home Mom and would be aware of her sons' every move. She would put her foot down if necessary. Once, when Carl told his mother that she was being unfair, she sat him down and told him that he was behaving like an ungrateful son and one day he would realize how lucky he was. As she left the room, she looked over her shoulder and said, "Carl, you live a blessed and privileged life. You have no idea what it's like to have real problems. Don't speak to me until you understand how lucky you are!" Carl felt humiliated, hurt, and angry. Where the hell was his father? Why was he stuck here alone all the time with this controlling bitch!!! Instantly he felt ashamed. Who was he to complain? He knew he was lucky to have this wonderful family and he knew his mother was right. Everyone loved and admired his mother, it must be him. He was behaving like a jerk. Eventually, Carl knew there was no choice but to apologize to his mother. When he did, she smiled and said "you're forgiven." Carl felt terrible about himself. In less than a year, he'd be in college, where he could to start his own life.

Exploring Intergenerational Patterns in Carl's Family

> *Carl's grandmother tried to hide her husband's drinking from the rest of the world. She went to great lengths to paint a picture of the perfect family. While their lives were ridden with confusion, chaos, and turbulence on a daily basis, Janeen's mother didn't seem to notice.*

1. Growing up in a household characterized by confusion, chaos, and turbulence effects everyone. How do you suspect it affected Janeen?
2. Any ideas as to what beliefs may have been forming in young Janeen's mind regarding her father's drinking?

> *Her mother snapped and told Janeen that she was ungrateful child who didn't know what it was like to have real problems. She told her that she was lucky to have all the things she had and to stop complaining. Janeen grew up believing that her needs were secondary to the image of the perfect family.*

1. How would you feel if you were Janeen when she asked her mother for help?
2. What do you think Janeen learned about sharing her feelings?
3. What conclusions do you think Janeen may have drawn about her family life?
4. Janeen believed that all of her problems during childhood were caused by alcohol. Can you see where this

belief may have developed? Might this be a little too simplistic view of a complicated family life?

> *Janeen had no fears about controlling her children as they entered adolescence. All it took was attention, structure, and high expectations. She sat Carl down and told him that he was behaving like an ungrateful son and one day he would realize how lucky he was. As she left the room, she looked over her shoulder and said, "Carl you live a blessed and privileged life. You have no idea what it's like to have real problems."*

1. Who does Janeen remind you of? (Hint: Take a look at her parents and her husband's parents.)
2. Even though Donald said he would never be the kind of father he had, notice who he married.
3. Janeen often felt alone during her childhood. Can you see how this pattern has repeated itself in her adult life with Donald?
4. How supportive can Donald be to his sons when he spends so much time at work? Where does this leave Carl and his brothers?
5. Does Carl's experience in college make more sense now?

CHAPTER 4:

Narcissistic Parents

Hopefully, you are beginning to see how beliefs are formed early in life and are directly associated with our needs. Human beings have a strong drive to *belong*, to make contributions, and to earn approval from our earliest teachers, our parents. Since our parents are also human beings with their own needs and desires, they may be rewarding what benefits them instead of meeting the needs of the child. All parents do this at times. But it is a matter of degree. The parents' own background and beliefs as well as life circumstances can draw attention away from their child in order to address the stressors that are directly affecting them.

But in families where one parent is narcissistic, there is no possibility for normal, day-to-day give and take. The "right way" of living is known only to the narcissistic parent and can change from moment to moment. There is no negotiation. The whole family lives every day on a constant state of alert, where everyone tries to focus on the needs and demands of this inconsistent and self-absorbed parent. Over time, a system is formed wherein the individual needs of each family member are subjugated to the demands of the narcissistic parent. In order to maintain stability in the family, members must keep a vigilant watch (for only the narcissistic knows what's right or wrong at any given moment). There is no room for individuality, experimentation, or the voicing of authentic feelings. If they are voiced, the child is identified as a problem child.

Children learn how to survive in such a system. One child may become reactive and start acting out, another may become over-sensitized to every cue and respond by meeting the needs of the narcissistic parent, and a third child may simply stay in the shadows. Since children are concrete thinkers; they are excellent soldiers in this militaristic group. If something is wrong, then something is wrong with *them;* the family's problems are *their* fault. These roles, when rigidly and inflexibly adhered to, can cause serious problems in our adult lives.

Carl, Mary, and Will grew up in families in which the needs of the parents were the focus of the family, and the children were expected to meet those needs. They were, in essence, recruited by their parents and held accountable for the family's emotional stability. Did you notice, for example, that the behavior of the children in our case studies were treated by their parents not in terms of what the *child* was experiencing or feeling, but of its impact on the *parents?* One parent seemed to dictate minute by minute how happy the household would be, based on his or her interpretation of the world at any given moment.

Over time, Mary, Carl, and Will learned that their needs were of little concern. When they asserted their own needs (that were in conflict with their parents' needs), they were often punished or ignored. They began to detach from their feelings and became the reflection of their parents' emotional needs. Both Carl and Mary grew physically into adults, but emotionally they were still stuck—they believed that they were worthless if they were not meeting the needs of those on whom they were dependent. You can see that both of these individuals were at a loss as to how to strike out as adults and claim their rightful place in the world. Neither Carl nor Mary had a clue as to how to heal because they had adopted a belief system where everything that was wrong was their fault. Will, on the other hand, came to the conclusion early in life that you "gotta take what you can get, don't ever show weakness, and screw the other guy before he screws you!"

CHAPTER 5:

Roles

"No man is an island, entire of itself"
John Donne, 1624[1]

By now, I hope that you can see that indeed no man is an island, and we all grew up in a system of highly sensitive connections with our family members. No one family member can be understood in isolation from another. You were not dropped onto earth from another planet in a pod; you grew up in a system, and each member of that system had a role to play and rules to respect.

The role you played in your family was influenced by many factors, including your own temperament, family stressors, birth order, your parents' needs and personalities, and your siblings' individual temperaments, as well as the roles they played. In healthy families, the system stays intact as individual members grow, change, and experiment. Members can assume any number of roles, based on their life circumstances. In unhealthy families, the stability of the system can be threatened by any member deviating from his assigned role. What would have happened to Mary's family, for example, if she had stopped caring for her little brothers? Imagine her parents' reaction if she lost interest in being an adult and started acting like the child she in fact was? Mary knew instinctively that she must stay in that caretaker role. She felt enormous (unspoken) pressure to reduce the level of anxiety in her family. There was no room, in her mind, for deviation. In addition, she was rewarded for her caretaking behavior

---

1   John Donne, *Devotions upon Emergent Occasions* (1623), XVII

and had natural organizational skills; she found joy in her tasks. This worked for her until she became an adult and was *only* comfortable when she was in a caretaking role. When searching for a mate, Mary might as well have worn that sign that said *I will take care of your needs at the expense of my own.* Listed below are some of the more common roles adopted by children who experience their family life as unpredictable, inconsistent, chaotic or frightening.

The Good Child (Also Known as the Hero)

- This is the child who assumes the role of holding up the family in an effort to portray the family as credible and functional to the outside world. The family hero is usually serious, focused, and driven. This child is often an exceptionally high achiever who is goal-oriented. Heroes are extra mature, usually following rules and regulations. They want to know the "right" way to do things. They believe that the solution to all of life's problems is hard work. They are often intolerant of feelings like sadness, shame, or anxiety, especially in themselves.

The Problem Child or Rebel (Also Known as the Scapegoat)

- Scapegoating within a family can lead to one child in a group of siblings being unfairly chosen as the "bad" child. This can lead to emotional and physical abuse of that child, often resulting in lifelong pain caused by this trauma. Over time, all of the family's problems may be blamed on the scapegoat.

The Caretaker

- This is the child who takes responsibility for the emotional well-being of the family. Caretakers try their best to hide the problems and protect the family's image. Very often, domestic duties such as cooking, cleaning and child rearing are also assumed by this person. This is the parents' role, of course, but in troubled families, it is this child who must step up to the plate.

The Lost Child

- This is the inconspicuous, quiet one whose needs are usually ignored or dismissed.

The Mascot

- This child uses comedy to divert attention away from family's anxiety. Many comedians report that this was their role in the family.

The Mastermind

- This child is the opportunist who capitalizes on the other family members' faults in order to get whatever he or she wants.

CHAPTER 6:

The Connection between Family Anxiety and Roles Assumed by the Children

The scapegoat receives so much negative focus that other siblings, by default, are a little freer. The parents ask, "What is wrong with this scapegoat child?" and over time the other children learn to ask the same question and to ascribe all of the family's problems to this one targeted child. This serves to reduce the family's anxiety because members of the family conclude (mistakenly) that "if only the scapegoat would stop screwing up, the family would be happy." It provides an answer and, thus, reduces anxiety. But the anxiety is still not being handled by the adults (where it belongs), so none of the children are totally free. For example, one child may stay out of the way to such a degree that he becomes invisible. This is the lost child. Another child may compete with the scapegoat or learn to be the opposite of the family "screw-up" in order to gain approval from the parents. This child may become the family hero, or the mastermind. A healthy family is characterized by strong boundaries between parents and children. The parents are the leaders, period. They shoulder the responsibility. A child in a healthy family system does not feel responsible for the emotional, physical, financial, or psychological well-being of the adults or his siblings. He is free to grow, learn, and experiment at each stage of his development, knowing he can count on his parents when he needs them.

Now, take some time and think about your own family. If you had siblings, what role did they play? What role did you play? Did you feel free to experiment with different roles? Did you worry about your parents? Describe your family during times of:

Anxiety
Conflict
Decision-making
Experimentation
Failures
Successes

CHAPTER 7:

Differentiation of Self

Differentiation of Self[2] is the process of freeing yourself from your family's processes in order to define yourself as a separate human being. This means being able to have opinions and values that may differ from your family members, while maintaining an emotional connection to them. Faced with an anxious situation, differentiated people are able to think things through and calmly reflect on a conflicted interaction afterward, realizing their own role in it and choosing a different response for the future.

Undifferentiated people, on the other hand, are easily moved to emotionality. They have difficulty separating feelings from thoughts. For example, when asked to think in anxious situations, they become flooded with feelings and tend to react emotionally. Asked what they think, they will report what they feel. Undifferentiated people have difficulty separating their own from other's feelings; they look to others to define how they should think about issues and interpret experiences.

Now, think back to your own childhood in terms of how differentiated you were allowed to be from your parents and other family members. Did you have a role to play? How much freedom did you feel to expand beyond this role?

- Were your needs and experiences addressed in terms of how they affected your life as an individual or in terms of how the family (or one particular family member) might have been affected?

---

2   Murray Bowen, *Family Therapy in Clinical Practice.* (Lanham, MD: Roman & Littlefield Publishers, Inc., 2004).

- What did each member do during times of stress? How did they line up?

- Did the needs of one person dictate how things must be in order to reduce anxiety in the family? In other words, did the family orbit around one central figure?

CHAPTER 8:

The Decision to Heal: Your Personal Story

Y*our* story is waiting to be told. Buy yourself a notebook or journal (or open up a fresh word processing document on your computer). Think of these blank pages as your life canvas awaiting your insights about your own family. Your beliefs are in there, and your healing begins with the first word you enter on your life canvas. Start writing your childhood story. As you write, remember that there is no "right" or "wrong" way to do this. Just start writing. Become a storyteller! Here are some helpful tips:

- Remember, no one will see this. No one is evaluating your story. No one is correcting your grammar or spelling. In short, no one is judging you!

- Take your time. If you get writer's block, don't force it. Some thoughts, memories, and feelings make take a while to bubble up.

- Use all the data you have so far (your insights as you read the case studies, your answers to questions, your reaction to the case studies).

- If it helps, make believe that you are writing about someone else. You can use the format I used when writing about Mary, Carl, and Will.

- Write in terms of feelings. Elaborate on your feelings. Be specific. Use rich, colorful language.

- Describe specific situations you remember about your childhood and your family's dynamics. Be sure to comment on how you felt during these times and what you believed.

- If you know anything about your parents' upbringing, start there. Talk about each of your parents and how they grew up.

- Based on the information you have or have heard through family stories, describe your grandparents and imagine what their lives might have been like.

- If possible, interview your parents and grandparents. (You can find some sample questions in the Appendix).

- Now imagine what beliefs each of your parents may have held when they had children. What were some of their possible beliefs at the time they met?

- It may help to draw your own family tree so the generations are visible.

- Discuss your siblings and where you fall in the birth order. Identify the role each of your siblings played. Comment on your relationship with them.

- Try different writing styles. Experiment, be flexible, and most importantly, do not judge!

- Allow the insights to rise to the surface. Keep writing!

- Write on the pages of this book, if that helps.

- Just for fun, pick a title for your family's drama (as you might for a movie or a play). In Carl's family, for example, the curtain rises on *The Perfect Family*. In Will's family, the title might be *Everybody Hates Dad!* And the title of Mary's family drama might be *The Good Girl*. What might the title of your family drama be?

CHAPTER 9:

The Courage to Change

Now that you have some clarity as to how your beliefs may have been formed and how those beliefs may be affecting your present-day behavior and choices, it is time to consider making some changes in the way you think, feel, and behave.

One way to begin to dig out of the hole—and to ultimately stay out—is to use that precious God-given gift: your own imagination. You can't go back in time, of course. But through your imagination, you will be able to see the past more clearly, more objectively. And what better way to practice than to play make believe?

Ladies and Gentlemen, I Present to You "The Do-Over!"

What if you could rewrite history? What would have happened if you had been able to *think through* some of your relationship dilemmas in the past rather than *reacting* anxiously to emotional demands and knee-jerk responses?

Let's start with Mary. With the stroke of a pen (actually a few clicks on a keyboard), I have rewritten Mary's story. Go back and reread Mary's original account of her whirlwind romance with Will (p. 1). Compare that account with the one below. What differences do you see in Mary's assumptions and beliefs?

Mary's New and Improved Assessment of Will

When we first met, I was very attracted to Will. He was kind, sweet, charming, and sexy. I must admit, I was smitten! He was so complimentary. I never felt as beautiful as when I was with Will. Then he started saying things that concerned me. He would tell me that I was the most loving person he had ever met. He asked me to help him learn to love fully so he could become a better person. He called me his "love teacher." I wondered how this could be true, since we had only met two weeks ago and, besides, how in the world could I teach another person to love? I didn't want the responsibility of being another person's "love teacher." He apparently had had a troubled childhood, and I was getting the sense that he expected me to fix it! (How in the world could I possibly do that?)

Will was recently divorced and had two little boys. He told me that he was seldom able to see his sons because his ex-wife started fights and it upset the children. This set off a red flag in my head. He seemed to be making an excuse (and blaming his ex-wife) for the fact that he was not seeing his sons. I thought to myself, "I don't like this. There's gotta be more to this story." He never missed an opportunity to compare me to his ex and to tell me how different I was from her. I was starting to feel manipulated. By our third date he was trashing his ex-wife (with a big smile on his face...creepy!). He said she was money-hungry and demanded exorbitant child-support payments. He knew she had just bought a new car, got to keep the beautiful house, and had a boyfriend who had lots of money. I noticed that our discussions were becoming more and more about his ex-wife and how unfair she was: another red flag! I had gathered enough information about this man; it was time for me to move on!

Mary's clear thinking and assessment during the early stages of her relationship with Will saved her years of heartache. In the revised scenario, Mary stepped back and evaluated what Will was saying *objectively.* She admitted that she was attracted to Will, but she didn't let that attraction distort her thoughts. Our new and improved Mary obviously had different beliefs about herself than the old Mary did. Her actions reflect these beliefs. For example:

1) The new and improved Mary assumed that she was a person of value, deserving of a healthy partner.
2) Although she wanted a man in her life and was very attracted to Will, she was able to stay calm and grounded so she could assess the facts.
3) Our new Mary made decisions based on a thought process that was not clouded by emotionality.
4) She did not allow herself to be manipulated by Will's considerable charm.

Notice that Mary did not choose to spend any more time with Will. She knew that it was far healthier to be alone and keep dating than it would be to enter a relationship with a man like Will.

CHAPTER 10:

Fear of Being Alone

A feeling deep in your soul, says you were half, now you're whole...
—from the song "People," sung by Barbra Streisand

Do you believe that you are only half a person until you meet your other half? Do you believe that you are incomplete without a life partner? Do you feel sorry for single people who wander the earth looking for their ideal mate? If so, beware; for your choosing mechanism is easily compromised by these beliefs. Instead of a rational, objective, open-minded approach to meeting someone, you enter the dating world feeling desperate, needy, empty, and fearful.

Think back to Mary. What state of susceptibility was she in when she met Will? Did you get the sense that Mary was just waiting for Will to come along? Did you notice how quickly she was willing to make this man her whole life, as if she was only a half a person until he came into her field of vision? Now compare *original* Mary to the *new and improved* Mary. Do you get the sense that new Mary is a whole person who is not driven by fear or emptiness as she listens to Will's story? Can you see her open-minded and cautious approach? Would you agree that new and improved Mary is looking for a partner, a teammate, and a friend—someone to compliment her, not consume her? The old Mary seems willing to toss her life aside to be replaced by Will's because she is afraid of being alone.

CHAPTER 11:

Parenting Yourself

When you were a child, you were powerless and could not survive alone. You were totally dependent on your caretakers, not only for food, shelter, and basic care, but for information about the world. They served as interpreters of all that you observed and experienced. If your caregivers were inconsistent, emotionally unavailable, anxious, or rejecting, you experienced the world as inconsistent and unpredictable: "I am hungry, wet, afraid, alone!" This early belief, established long before you even had language, could be the basis for your fears in the present day.

Close your eyes and imagine a particular time in your childhood when you really needed the help of an adult. Now imagine your adult-self taking the hand of that innocent child. Imagine the adult-you stepping into this situation and taking charge on behalf of the child-you. Imagine holding, rocking, comforting, and loving this child. Have a dialogue with this little you:

The Child-You: I am scared. I can't do this!
The Adult-You: Don't worry, little one. I am here now to protect and help you. I am an adult. I have power, ideas, skills, and resources that we didn't have when we were little. I won't let anything happen to you, and I am always here to help with your problems. There is no problem too big for me. You are a loving, beautiful person, and together we will get through this. Now let's go solve this problem!

Can you feel your heart softening? Can you see in your mind, how vulnerable and lovable you were; how sweet and perfect?

Can you also see the difference between the power of an adult and the powerlessness of a child? As an adult, you have tremendous power—the power to support yourself in every way. So rather than feeling loss because you may not have had parents who were there for you or who let you down in some way, remember: you can parent yourself; you can quell the fears of that little child inside you.

CHAPTER 12:

Getting Better Through Insight

When you were a child, you did not have the capacity for insight or abstract thinking. But now that you are an adult, you can go back and at least *see* things in a new light. You have already begun to collect data that may change the way you see your childhood—the role you may have played in your family drama, your parents' relationship with each other, intergenerational patterns, and your childhood beliefs. You might also begin to identify how these patterns are playing out in your adult life.

Now what if, by using this data, you could reframe your childhood or open up options for evaluating your life differently? What if you could step back and look at your family dynamics from a more objective, informed perspective? Let's look at how Carl's story might have been told. Go back and reread Carl's original story on page 23. Like Mary, take note of the differences:

Carl's New and Improved Family Story

As I look back over my childhood years, I can see now that, although everything looked perfect on the surface, there were lots of strong, negative feelings lying beneath the façade of our "perfect" family. Don't get me wrong, my brothers and I were well cared for and privileged in many ways. I did well academically and excelled in several sports. My brothers and I received a lot of attention, that's for sure. In fact, my mother never took her eyes off us. She was what some might refer to as a "helicopter mom" always hovering over us. To the outside world she appeared cool, calm, and collected. But on the inside my mother was so tightly wound that we all knew to stay in line or else. My father was never around. When he finally did come home from work, he would step lightly, searching for evidence of what her mood might be at that moment. If she was in a bad mood, he would disappear to the garage or go back to his office. I can't say I blame him.

When I headed out for college, I didn't realize that I was totally unprepared. Even though I worked hard at school and always had a part-time job, I didn't realize that, up until that point, everything had been done for me. I can remember my mother decorating the dorm, hanging my clothes and lining my socks and underwear neatly in the drawers. She has lists upon lists. The last thing she said to me was, "Now Carl, don't fall back into your old habits. I know you are basically lazy and sloppy…just kidding sweetheart. I just want you to succeed." The thought of her leaving me there was terrifying, although I didn't admit this to anyone, especially myself!

During my first semester at college I was depressed. I mistakenly believed that, once I was free of my mother's rules, I'd be able to enjoy a happy, carefree life. Not so. I began drinking, and smoking a lot of pot. I started missing classes and soon my grades plummeted, I felt lost.

It was during this hazy, unhappy time, that I met Ashley. It didn't take long before Ashley began making small, critical remarks. She'd say things like "No wonder your previous girlfriend dumped you" and "God, comb your hair once in a while" or "when I first met you, I thought you were adorable, now not so much."

I started seeing the school counselor and he helped me to see the similarities between Ashley and my mother. I was shocked to discover that I had very low self-esteem, and startled to realize that there was no coincidence to the fact that I hooked up with Ashley. Before counseling, I would have never seen these connections. The counselor was the first one to point out that maybe my childhood wasn't so "perfect" after all and that some of the patterns I had developed in childhood were carrying over into adulthood. He helped me to understand how toxic my relationship was with Ashley and I was not a victim. I had choices.

Chapter 13:

Out of the Past and into the Present

At this point you may be thinking, "That was fun, but I'm still here and I can't change my life with the stroke of a pen or the click of a keyboard!" Of course that's true. But you can begin to see your present life differently and then move forward, slowly making small changes in the here and now. These changes will be scary at first. In all likelihood you will feel guilty, uncomfortable, or anxious. But the only way around it is through it. And for goodness sakes, don't take on the scariest person right off the bat! Pick a coworker, a stranger on a bus, or perhaps someone at the grocery store. Try to remember a recent encounter with someone from which you walked away feeling pretty miserable about yourself. Perhaps you agreed to do something you didn't want to do, or maybe you didn't speak up when it was your right to do so. Pick a situation where you reacted as if by a knee-jerk response, as if you were *programmed* to react this way.

Remember, when you do not *think through* your responses to relationship dilemmas but rather *react* anxiously to perceived, emotional demands, old patterns of behavior will be called upon instead of thoughtful, objective, open-minded solutions to the present day-problems.

Here's an example of a "knee-jerk response of my own. This is a true account of a situation that occurred a few years ago.

I had made arrangements to provide some technical assistance to a group of coworkers. Unfortunately, I had not written it down in my day planner. On the day of the workshop, I received a call asking, "Where are you?" As soon as I heard my colleague's voice, I remembered! In an instant, I began to cough and said, "I am so sorry, I'm sick today and I need to go home. I was just about to call you!" At least ten people had rearranged their schedules to be at this workshop. I felt terrible for my mistake, but I felt worse about my response. I had lied without even thinking—the lie had rolled right off my tongue. My colleague, of course, assured me that she understood and wished me a speedy recovery. I had to go home to keep up the façade. To this day, this encounter remains a painful, humiliating memory for me. Why had I lied? I had obviously reacted by regressing to old patterns of behavior. It didn't take but an instant, and I had a whole "I feel sick" scenario to fall back on. The connection to my own family's pattern of lying to avoid being shamed, exposed, or ridiculed was played out in this otherwise typical day at work.

Now, your assignment is to rewrite this encounter for me. Clearly, I had made a mistake and forgotten an important meeting. But that is not why I still feel so terrible about this situation when I look back. I did not feel good about lying, and I still cringe when I think of this, even today. What kind of response do you think might have left me feeling better about the situation and better about myself? Take a little time and rewrite this unfortunate episode in my life. If I had taken the time to think from the point of view of my principles instead of reacting anxiously, what might have been my response?

Next, pick a real-life scenario in your own adult life, one where you walked away feeling dissatisfied, empty, or ashamed of your reaction. Write it down. Then take a long look at your own knee-jerk response.

- How did you handle the dilemma?

- Did you feel a sense of powerlessness during the interaction?

- Postulate some possible family patterns associated with your response. Whose face do you see when you think about these patterns?

After making some connections to your childhood and to possible learned patterns, rewrite your scenario. Make the ending one in which you end up feeling proud instead of ashamed. Be sure to comment on the feelings related to your *new and improved* response.

CHAPTER 14

Healthy Thoughts vs. Emotional Reactions

Imagine Carl sitting in his counselor's office at college. He is describing an interaction he had with his father on a recent fishing trip. He is still fuming. With frustration and fury, Carl reports the interaction to his counselor.

Carl: It's so hard to talk to Mom.
Donald: Don't criticize your mother, Carl. She does so much for you boys, and she's had a hard life.
Carl: Why do you always do that, Dad? You stick up for her no matter what!
Donald: No need to shout, son. I'm just trying to tell you—
Carl (interrupts): Forget I ever brought it up.

It is obvious to see why Carl feels frustrated. Chances are Carl and his dad will leave this encounter feeling sad, angry, frustrated, and/or misunderstood.

Now, the rewrite:
(Take note that it is *not* Donald who changes, but Carl.)

Carl: It's so hard to talk to Mom.
Donald: Don't criticize your mother, Carl. She does so much for you boys, and she's had a hard life.
Carl: Tell me about her life.

Donald: Well, her father was an alcoholic; he was a great guy when he was sober but a real S.O.B. when he was drinking.

Carl: What was he like when he was drinking? How did he treat Mom?

Can you see the difference here? Carl has resisted the urge toward his usual knee-jerk response. He doesn't react emotionally but thinks through his options in order to get more information from his father about his mother. He chooses to focus on learning rather than getting angry at his father.

CHAPTER 15:

You Can Change. It Is Possible!

Albert Ellis, founder of Rational Emotive Therapy (RET), believed that human emotions do not magically exist but are the direct result of thoughts, beliefs, ideas, and attitudes.[3] Ellis proposed that we create our feelings by inserting catastrophic thoughts between the original happening and the ensuing feeling.

Ellis postulates that our crippling feelings are a direct result of the *thought* that we automatically insert, *not the happening itself*, and that if we could learn to simply change the thought, the result would be different feelings—in all likelihood more positive ones. Let's look at Carl's conversation with his dad in chapter 14 when they were talking on the boat.

The originating comment by Donald: Don't criticize your mother, Carl. She does so much for you boys, and she's had a hard life.

Carl's intervening thought: I am getting nowhere! I will never ever be able to talk to either one of my parents. It's hopeless!

Carl's feelings: hurt, anger, frustration, hopelessness, leading to his response: "Forget it!"

---

3   Albert Ellis, Robert Harper. *A Guide to Rational Living.* North Hollywood, CA: Wilshire Book Company, 1975.

Now, here's the rewrite:

Donald: Don't criticize your mother, Carl. She does so much for you boys, and she's had a hard life.

Carl's new and improved thoughts: If I want to learn more about my family, I have to keep the conversation flowing and not react emotionally. **Carl feels calm and in control.**

Carl's response: "Tell me about her life."

As Carl listens to his father describe his mother's past, he can see the pain in his father's face. He can see what a good man his father is. Carl's heart softens and he sees and hears so much more than he would have if he had reacted with frustration. The door is now open. Carl's father feels listened to and safe. He is much more likely to keep talking.

So if *the intervening thought* is the pivotal and controlling factor in your overall sense of well-being, then the simple formula is *Change your thinking, change your feelings!* You can make the *choice* to be happy or miserable. You can make the *choice* to suffer or not suffer, and you have the ability to *choose* from an infinite range of responses rather than the old, worn-out, knee-jerk responses you might otherwise make.

How often do you just react using the old patterns of communication with your parents, friends, siblings, or coworkers instead of actively changing these patterns? How often do you respond without thinking? How often do you ask for information about their thoughts and feelings and about their lives?

CHAPTER 16:

How to Handle the Narcissist(s) in Your Life

Ah, now we take on the big guns! Chances are, the narcissist(s) in your life will not be happy with the *new and improved* you. Be prepared for this. Since narcissists think in terms of *I want what I want, when I want it,* your first attempts to negotiate *your* needs won't go smoothly. Remember, you have been a participant in this dynamic, so expect some shock and resistance when you start behaving differently. Think of it this way: If you've always given in to the tantrums of a toddler, she will *not* be happy when you start to set limits. In fact, her tantrums may escalate. The same is true of narcissistic people. In order to get things back to normal, they may try every trick in the book (guilt, manipulation, maneuvering, and even bullying) to get what they want.

Let's take a look at an example. Tomorrow is Sunday, and you have been looking forward to a day to yourself, just padding around the house, spending the day alone with a good book. Your friend Joan has just lost her job and has broken up with yet another boyfriend. Since Joan is narcissistic, you often walk away from interactions with her thinking, "Why did I say yes when I clearly wanted to say no?" or "Why didn't I stand up for myself?"

Normally, your conversation might go something like this:

Joan: I need to get out of the house! Let's go shopping to-morrow. I'll pick you up at nine o'clock. We'll have breakfast and then hit the mall!

Your intervening thought: Well, she has been lonely and bored since she lost her job. And on top of that, her boyfriend broke up with her. I shouldn't be so selfish. This is a difficult time for Joan. I should be a better friend. What's the big deal? I'll just go.

Your response: "OK." (Not surprisingly, you later feel resentment and anger at your friend *and* at yourself. As you are getting dressed the next day to go shopping, you mumble to yourself about how weak you are and how pushy Joan is.)

In fact, Joan is very hard to say no to, and as you look back, you realize that you have a pattern of giving in to her. But you have decided that it's time for change. Her friendship is important to you, and you don't want to just toss it away because of harbored feelings of frustration or resentment. You have made the choice to do your part in striking a better balance in your friendship with Joan.

You tell Joan you do not want to go shopping, mentioning your desire to have a restful day at home by yourself. You are not surprised by her response. But this time, you are putting your needs on an even playing field with Joan's needs.

The new and improved version:

Joan begins the push to get what she wants: Ah, c'mon. You can rest when we get home from shopping. We'll make it a short day.

Your intervening thought: I am not surprised by her reaction. This happens most of the time. I really do need a day at home tomorrow to rest and recharge my batteries. I am holding my ground.

Your response: I'm sorry you're feeling so miserable, Joan, really I am, but I need a day off just to rest and hang around in my pajamas. I don't want to go out anywhere tomorrow. (You are feeling very proud and confident right now.)

But remember, narcissists are not interested in what *you* want or need. It's all about *them*. So chances are Joan will not give up so quickly. The push continues:

Joan's response: OK. I'll come over and hang out at your house.
Your intervening thought: Wow, she's good! She's not giving up. But I really do need this day off by myself. I am holding my ground.
Your response: Joan, right now our needs are conflicting. I need a day just to myself, and you need to spend time with friends. But I really need this, so I'm going to say no, not tomorrow; another day for sure.

Joan may *up the ante:*

Joan's response: Thanks a lot. I thought you were my friend. You know how awful my life is right now!
Your intervening thought: The idea that I am not a good friend because I need one day to myself is not rational. I will not hook to this manipulation.
Your response: (Ignoring the comment about the friendship) Joan, I'm not going out anywhere, and I'm going to spend the day alone.

Joan may not give up, and this type of interchange may go on and on. (This dynamic is very familiar to me, and I can feel the urge, even as I'm writing this, to give in to Joan!) But good emotional health is a choice. Joan may get angry, she may pout. She may even show up at your doorstep tomorrow. The narcissist is a formidable opponent in the tug of war that ensues when your needs conflict with his or her needs. So prepare! Think of all the possibilities and how you'll handle them. Most importantly, *think clearly and resist the urge to react emotionally.* Anger, hurt, and disbelief are common feelings when reality hits. Resist the urge to act on these feelings.

Emotional reactions may feel good in the moment, especially if you have been harboring resentment and you want to let all that hurt and anger out, but in the end, emotional responses tend to cloud what is really going on in your relationship with the narcissist. The two of you have developed a pattern in which the narcissist demands and you comply. This pattern has played itself out over and over. Ending this dynamic with assertive, thoughtful responses will free you to see your relationship more clearly and determine your next move.

CHAPTER 17:

What If the Narcissist in My Life Doesn't Come Around?

Changing the dynamic with the narcissist in your life may become a difficult and draining undertaking. You may find (as I did) that the narcissistic person simply cannot adapt. He or she cannot understand the concept of negotiation and may become hostile, aggressive, or even more manipulative than ever! You may find yourself blamed for ruining the relationship. In desperation, the narcissist may make promises to change, but over time you might observe things slipping back into familiar patterns. You may finally admit that this relationship is not nourishing in any way. It is, in fact, terribly difficult, draining, and toxic.

As your awareness increases, so might your sadness. It is extremely difficult to admit that this person will never meet even your most basic needs. In many ways, this loss is like a death. Let yourself mourn the loss. What has died is hope, and that is a powerful loss. Let yourself grieve. Be kind to yourself. You are not responsible for the self-absorbed nature of the narcissist. But you owe it to yourself to invest your energies in more fruitful and loving relationships. You can make this choice. You are worth it. There are others out there who have an enormous capacity for love and giving. Find them and start living the life you deserve!

EPILOGUE:

Some Final Thoughts

If you have identified a person in your life who is narcissistic, hopefully this book has helped to provide clarity and hope in your quest to develop healthier relationships and a more peaceful life. I wish you well, and I can tell you from personal experience that this is a journey well worth taking. If you are like me, you will start to see narcissists everywhere. You'll spot them instantly. When you first meet someone, take notice of how many questions they ask about you, their level of curiosity about *your* life versus how often they talk about themselves (and how often they use the word *I*). This little trick has helped me to spot narcissists early and to politely disengage. Usually your first instincts are correct. Trust yourself. Just because you have been snagged by a narcissist in the past doesn't mean you are doomed to make the same choices in the future. And as you grow and begin to expand your circle of friends and loved ones, remember the words of Maya Angelou, "When people show you who they are, believe them, the first time."

Questions to Ask Your Parents and Grandparents

If you are lucky enough to have your parents and/or your grandparents alive and well, don't miss this opportunity to interview them. Years ago, as a course assignment, I interviewed my parents, and to this day, our conversation remains one of my most precious memories. And boy did I learn about them: their beliefs, their own memories and perceptions, their respective views on their life together. I was nervous at first, but once they started talking, they couldn't stop. As I look back on that day, sitting across from my parents at the picnic table, I believe they enjoyed it too. Here are some questions that may be helpful in getting the conversation going. Pick and choose those that will work for you.

1. Where were you born?
2. How did your family come to live there?
3. Were there other family members in the area? Who?
4. How was your name chosen?
5. Describe the house you grew up in.
6. What is your earliest childhood memory?
7. Describe your family members.
8. What was school like for you as a child?
9. Who were your childhood heroes?

10. What were your favorite songs and music?
11. Did you have pets? Did you have a favorite pet?
12. Who were your friends when you were growing up?
13. Describe your family holidays. Did your family have special traditions?
14. Do you remember your grandparents? Describe the oldest relative you remember as a child.
15. Are there any stories about particular family members who stand out?
16. Are there any physical characteristics that run in your family?
17. How did you meet? What did you do on dates?
18. Who proposed?
19. Where and when did you get married?
20. What memory stands out the most from your wedding day?
21. What were the early days of your marriage like?
22. What were the early days of parenthood like?
23. Why did you choose your children's names/nicknames?
24. What are a few of your best memories with your children?
25. What did you want to be when you grew up?

Bibliography

Bowen, Murray. *Family Therapy in Clinical Practice*. Lanham, MD: Roman & Littlefield Publishers, Inc., 2004.

Chopra, Deepak. *Power, Freedom, and Grace*. San Rafael, CA: Amber-Allen Publishing, Inc., 2006.

Ellis, Albert, and Robert Harper. *A Guide to Rational Living*. North Hollywood, CA: Wilshire Book Company, 1975.

Gilbert, Roberta. *The Eight Concepts of Bowen Theory*. Falls Church, VA: Leading Systems Press, 2004, 2006.

Jeffers, Susan, *Feel the Fear and Do It Anyway*. New York: Ballantine Books Trade Paperback Edition, 2007.

McGoldrick, Monica, and Randy Gerson. *Genograms in Family Assessment*. New York: WW. Norton and Company, 1985.

Pressman, Stephanie-Donald, and Robert M. Pressman. *The Narcissistic Family*. San Francisco: Josey-Bass, 1994.

Smith, Manuel J., *When I Say No, I Feel Guilty: How to Cope—Using the Skills of Systematic Assertive Therapy*. New York: Dial Press, 1975.